Anaxagoras
and the Origin
of Panspermia Theory

Anaxagoras and the Origin of Panspermia Theory

Margaret R. O'Leary

iUniverse, Inc.
New York Bloomington Shanghai

Anaxagoras and the Origin of Panspermia Theory

iUniverse books may be ordered through booksellers or by contacting:

iUniverse
1663 Liberty Drive
Bloomington, IN 47403
www.iuniverse.com
1-800-Authors (1-800-288-4677)

Because of the dynamic nature of the Internet, any Web addresses or links contained in this book may have changed since publication and may no longer be valid.

ISBN: 978-0-595-49596-2 (pbk)
ISBN: 978-0-595-61166-9 (ebk)

Printed in the United States of America

To Catherine W. Brown

Excerpt from Trial of Socrates

Meletus: Yes; I say that you disbelieve in gods altogether.

Socrates: You surprise me, Meletus; what is your object in saying that? Do you suggest that I do not believe that the sun and the moon are gods, like other men do?

Meletus: He certainly does not, gentlemen of the jury, since he says that the sun is a stone and the moon a mass of earth.

Socrates: Do you imagine that you are prosecuting Anaxagoras, my dear Meletus? Have you so poor an opinion of these gentlemen, and do you assume them to be so illiterate as not to know that the writings of Anaxagoras of Clazomenae are full of theories like these? And do you seriously suggest that it is from me that the young get these ideas, when they can buy them on occasion in the orchestra for a drachma at most, and so have the laugh on Socrates if he claims them for his own, especially when they are so peculiar? Tell me honestly, Meletus, is that your opinion of me? Do I believe in no god?

Meletus: No, none at all; not in the slightest degree.

Plato's *Apology* 26d–e

Contents

Preface

My interest in antiquity was first awakened by Will Durant's *The Life of Greece*, a gift from a friend during my time as a student at Smith College in Northampton, Massachusetts. Subsequent degrees in religion, zoology, and medicine, followed by time spent earning a living and raising a family, postponed my scholarly study of antiquity until now—thirty-six years later.

Anaxagoras and the Origin of Panspermia Theory explains an ancient natural philosopher's revolutionary idea about the origin of life. Ionian philosopher Anaxagoras' obsession with natural science and his utter rejection of supernatural explanations for happenings in the physical universe violated venerated religious norms held by Athenian society. Indeed, his criticism of the belief that humans could tease, flatter, enrage, seduce, chastise, and bargain with their gods to manipulate outcomes almost earned him a cup of hemlock, poured straight up by the Athenian multitude. This study of Anaxagoras' theory of panspermia portrays the initial collision between science and religion in the fifth century BC.

This monograph is the first of a series that tracks the theory of panspermia from its origin in the fifth century BC to the development of its modern counterpart, astrobiology.

MRO
February 2008
Saint Charles, Illinois

1. Anaxagoras' Theory of Panspermia

The theory of *panspermia* postulates that an infinite number of cosmic "seeds" continuously fall onto Earth and other cosmic bodies to yield "life" when conditions are ripe. The theory dates back at least twenty-five hundred years to Anaxagoras, the august Greek philosopher, born in 500 BC in Clazomenae, Ionia.[1] Anaxagoras was the first philosopher to use the neuter-gender noun *sperma* (Greek for "something sown" or "seed") to explain the origin of life on Earth and, he posited, other worlds.[2]

The word *Greek* is the Roman name for the people of Greece. The Greeks of the post-Homeric period were known as *Hellenes*. Homer most often referred to the Greeks as *Achaeans*, or *Achaians*, and to Greece as *Achaia*.[3]

Anaxagoras' theory of panspermia survived a perilous intellectual journey following his death in 428 BC, yet it survives today as astrobiology, the scientific study of life in the universe, including its origin, evolution, distribution, and future on Earth and other cosmic bodies.[4] This monograph describes the life of Anaxagoras and the content of the panspermia theory he espoused, using sources that include *testimonia* and *ipsissima verba*.

2. Anaxagoras Sources

Modern knowledge of the ideas of Anaxagoras and other so-called Presocratic philosophers is astonishingly recent in Western thought, emerging only in the late nineteenth century AD. In 1897, for example, American classicist Arthur Fairbanks (1864–1944) wrote, "The Hegelian School and in particular [German philosopher and historian of philosophy Eduard] Zeller [1814–1908] have shown us the place of the earlier thinkers in the history of Greek thought, and the importance of a knowledge of their work for all who wish to understand Plato and Aristotle."[5]

German classicist Hermann Diels (1848–1922) located and assembled numerous short fragments of the Presocratic philosophers' writings, including those "preserved by later writers and accounts of these thinkers' opinions, given mainly by Aristotle."[5]

Anaxagoras qualifies as a Presocratic philosopher, though barely so, as his life and the life of Socrates overlapped. Anaxagoras wrote only one known book, which has been lost; however, *fragments* of the book have survived as quotations in the *testimonia* of Simplicius and Sextus Empiricus, among others, which Diels collected and aggregated along with the extant materials of the other Presocratic philosophers.[6–9] The first "admirable critical edition of Diels (Berlin, 1879) was a compilation of the *Greek text* [italics added] of the doxographists," noted Fairbanks in 1897.[5] To learn about Anaxagoras' ideas at the end of the nineteenth century, one needed to know how to read Greek.

Fairbanks followed Diels' lead by preparing an English edition of the extant quotes of the Presocratic philosophers. Fairbanks wrote the following about his work, *The First Philosophers of Greece*:

> In the present work it has been my plan to prepare for the student a *Greek text* [italics added] of the fragments of these early philosophers which shall represent as accurately as possible the results of recent scholarship, and to add such critical notes as may be necessary to enable the scholar to see on what basis the text rests. From this text I [Fairbanks] have prepared a *translation of the fragments into English* [italics added], and along with this a translation of the important passages bearing on these early thinkers in Plato and Aristotle, and in the Greek doxographists as collected by Diels, in order that the student of early Greek thought might have before him in compact form practically all the materials on which the history of this thought is to be based.[5]

In Fairbanks' book the original Greek is reproduced on the left-hand page, and the English translation is on the right-hand page. The book contains fragments and *testimonia* for Thales, Anaximandros, Anaximenes, Herakleitos, Xenophanes, Parmenides, Zeno, Melissos, Pythagoras and the Pythagoreans, Empedocles, and Anaxagoras.[5] The segments of the book corresponding to each of the philosophers listed above are available online as a part of the Hanover Historical Texts Project.[10]

Five years after Fairbanks published his book, Diels published (1903) *Die Fragmente der Vorsokratiker* [*The Fragments of the Presocratics*], which contained fragments and *testimonia* about Anaxagoras and the other Presocratic philosophers. Diels revised and expanded his work three times, completing four editions in all. Walther Kranz edited a fifth edition (1934–7) and a sixth edition (1952). The Diels-Kranz work includes all the known works of the Presocratics. Many scholars consider it the standard reference in the field of ancient philosophy.

Diels-Kranz (DK) assigned a number to each Presocratic philosopher and divided each philosopher's works into three groups:

A. *Testimonia*: ancient accounts of the author's life and doctrines;

B. *Ipsissima verba*: the exact words of the author, i.e., "fragments"; and

C. Imitations: works that take the author as a model.[11]

In 1948 classicist Kathleen Freeman published *Ancilla to the Pre-Socratic Philosophers*, which is a "complete translation [into English] of the fragments of the Pre-Socratic philosophers given in Diels, *Die Fragmente der Vorsokratiker*, Fifth Edition (B-sections)."[12] Freeman limited her comments on the readings and interpretation to footnotes and referred her readers to her *Companion to the Pre-Socratic Philosophers* to which the *Ancilla* was considered ancillary.

In 2007 classicist Patricia Curd focused solely on Anaxagoras in *Anaxagoras of Clazomenae* by providing fragments, *testimonia* containing fragments, *testimonia not* containing fragments, and a series of essays about main issues in Anaxagoras cosmogony. In part 1 of her book, Curd reproduced, on each left-hand page in the original Greek, a DK Anaxagoras *B* passage from *Simplicius, on Aristotle's Physics*. On the opposite page, she translated the Greek text into the corresponding English of Simplicius' passage, in a manner reminiscent of Fairbanks, for example:

- Left-hand page (p. 14): DK number B1 155.23: Passage contains quotation of Anaxagoras in the original Greek, from *Simplicius on Aristotle's Physics*.

- Right-hand page (p.15): B1: Passage contains quotation of Anaxagoras translated into English, from *Simplicius on Aristotle's Physics*, as follows:

Anaxagoras says that the homogeneous stuffs, unlimited in amount, are separated off from a single mixture, with all things being in everything but each being characterized by what predominates. He makes this clear in the first book of the *Physics*, when he says at the beginning, "*All things were together, unlimited both in amount and in smallness, for the small, too, was unlimited. And because all things were together, nothing was evident on account of smallness; for air and aether covered all things, both being unlimited, for these are the greatest among all things both in amount and in largeness.*"[13]

The italics in the passage immediately above identify the Anaxagoras quote, distinguishing it from the rest of the text, which belongs to Simplicius.

Cleve, Cornford, Curd, Schofield, Sider, Vlastos, and other modern English-language Anaxagoras scholars have used Anaxagoras fragments and *testimonia* to reconstruct the philosophy of this man in *their own testimonia*, which (like earlier *testimonia*) are limited by the paucity of original material and each writer's personal point of view.[14–19] For example, the eminent scholar Cleve approached his reconstruction not by fitting together, like pieces of a jigsaw puzzle, stray fragments into a literary whole, but by constructing "*a philosophic building in such a way that all the authentic material handed down can be fitted in* [italics by Cleve]."[20] The reader must take on faith Cleve's assertion that he accomplished his stated goal.

The point here is that Anaxagoras sources are old, invariably complex, and seldom complete; thus the interpretations of these sources must be cautiously assessed to determine their reliability and validity. Fairbanks noted more than a century ago that one can rely on scholars who trace the history of the development of thought among the earlier Greek thinkers, or one can "go behind these accounts and examine the evidence for himself."[5]

3. The Ionians

The Ionians were "East Greeks" (as contrasted with "European Greeks") who inhabited the west coast including offshore islands of what today is Turkey.[21] Cook posits that in antiquity the East Greeks comprised the *Aeolians* in the north, *Ionians* in the middle, and *Dorians* in the south along the west coast of present-day Turkey.[21] Early in the Iron Age, the Ionian migration began from the western Aegean shores of Attica and Argolis to the eastern Aegean shores of Ionia. Cook describes the character of the Ionian migration:

> This seems not to have been an officially planned operation, but a sequence of private ventures, not necessarily of similar size or character. Dating is difficult, since it depends on finds in the settlements, and so far, excavation has not been extensive or lucky; but the current opinion is that the migration began in the later eleventh century [BC] and may have continued for a hundred years or more. Internal migration, that is the foundation of new settlements by established ones, went on much longer. The legends, recorded or invented in later times, are all more or less untrustworthy.[22]

The early Ionian migrants encountered no powerful native states in western Anatolia.[23] Still, the Ionians spread inland from the sea no more than twenty-five miles up the big-river valleys. By the seventh century BC more than twenty major cities existed. Miletus (Miletos), the greatest Ionian city, has received the most archaeological attention.[24–25]

These major cities—Ionian, Aeolian, and Dorian—each had "their own federation, effective in ceremonial matters, but hardly interfering in the neighbourly wars so characteristic of the Greek *polis*," notes Cook.[22] For example, twelve Ionian cities formed a confederation known as the Ionian (or Panionic) Dodecapolis (or League) as early as 800 BC, according to

Ionian historian Herodotus (484–425 BC).[25] The cities were Miletus, Myus, Priene, Ephesus, Colophon, Lebedus, Teos, Erythrae, Clazomenae, Phocaea, Chios, and Samos. Residents of these twelve cities spoke dialects of a common Ionian language. Herodotus writes about their unique Ionian dialects, as follows:

> There are four different dialects of the Ionic language, distributed as follows: the most southerly of the Ionian towns is Miletus, with Myrus [*sic*] to the north of it, and then Priene, these three being in Caria and speaking the same dialect. Ephesus, Colophon, Lebedus, Teos, Erythrae, Clazomenae, and Phocaea are in Lydia, and share a common dialect completely distinct from what is spoken at the places previously mentioned. There are three other Ionian settlements, two being the islands of Samos and Chios and one, Erythrae, a mainland town. The two latter use the same dialect, Samos a peculiar one of its own.[26]

The twelve cities came together during the Panionia, a religious festival and athletic competition, in a sanctuary called Panionium at the foot of the mountain opposite the island of Samos. The site was "chosen by common consent of the Ionians and dedicated to Poseidon," wrote Herodotus.[26–27] The Panionium was not originally a political or military organization. For example, Gorman notes, "When the Lydians attacked the cities of Asia Minor [as discussed below], there was no sign of any collective response."[28]

The kingdom of Lydia, with its capital at Sardis about fifty miles inland from Smyrna, captured the Ionian cities, except Miletus, around 550 BC. Several years later (547 BC), Persia annexed Lydia and reconquered the Ionian cities. Neither Lydian nor Persian rule was harsh, however, and the Ionian cities continued to prosper. Then, in 499 BC, the East Greeks *did* unite against the Persians in the so-called Ionian Revolt, sacked Sardis, and in 494 BC lost to the Persians in a naval battle off Miletus.[29] The Persians responded in kind by ruthlessly razing Miletus, "the jewel of Ionia." Fifteen years later (479 BC), Athens repelled the Persian invasion of European Greece and proceeded to liberate—then subjugate—the islands and coastal cities of Ionia.[30]

The Ionians "had the good fortune to establish their settlements in a region, which enjoys a better climate than any other we know of," wrote Herodotus in the fifth century BC.[30] "It does not resemble what is found either further north, where there is an excess of cold and wet, or further south, where the weather is both too hot and too dry." In other words, Ionia was moist and warm.[31] In addition, many of the Ionian cities rested on the deep alluvial soil of the broad river valleys and on the coastal strip of deep soils resulting from erosion of the Stephania Hills escarpment of Ionia. Thus they were ideal for Mediterranean-type agricultural polyculture.

Ancient Ionians (including Anaxagoras, a landowner and farmer) planted fields of barley, wheat, and millet—the one-seeded cereal grasses. They also nurtured grapevines for making raisins and wine and cultivated olives, figs, and lentils.[32] Archaeologists working in Ionia—both on land and offshore excavating rare shipwrecks dating to the fifth century BC—have found hundreds of ancient amphorae, some of which contain carbonized seeds that suggest the substances they carried, for example, grapes.[33–36] The Ionians also raised goats and sheep and were famous for their woolen products, which they traded abroad.

Ionian communities did not, "except at Gela and Siris, start colonizing overseas before the mid-seventh century, and then it was northward—the Aegean coast of Thrace, Propontis and, a little before 600 [BC], the Black Sea (or Pontus)," notes Cook.[32] The reasons for colonization differed from city to city and are multifold, including "land hunger" (need for more arable land), need for natural resources (for example, silver, gold, and tin and copper to make bronze), and trade in "raw wool, hides, timber, fish, hemp, flax, honey, and probably slaves" throughout the Mediterranean.

The Ionians, according to Durant, were unique:

> Taking a lesson from the Phoenicians and gradually bettering their instruction, Ionian merchants established colonies as trading posts in Egypt, Italy, the Propontis, and the Euxine [Black Sea]. Miletus alone had eighty such colonies, sixty of them in the north. From Abydos, Cyzicus, Sinope, Olbia, Trapezus, and Dioscurias, Miletus drew flax, timber, fruit, and metals, and paid for these with the products of her

handicrafts. The wealth and luxury of the city became a proverb and a scandal throughout Greece. Milesian merchants, overflowing with profits, lent money to enterprises far and wide, and to the municipality itself. They were the Medici of the Ionian Renaissance.[37]

Ionians from the cities of Phocaea, Miletus, or perhaps both, founded Lampsacus (Lampsakos), a colony at the northeast corner of the Hellespont, the ancient name of the narrow strait now known as the Dardanelles.[38] Anaxagoras fled from Athens to Lampsacus to avoid execution, dying there in 428 BC (more below).

4. Hellenic Religion

Hellenes explained the origin and nature of their world through the activities of anthropomorphic gods and demigods, as described elsewhere.[39–40] "The gods were mainly immortal men and women, incomparably more powerful than mortals, but like mortals susceptible to all human emotions and appetites," notes Lattimore.[41] But gods were also *forces*, such as Ares, who *was* war (*ares*) and Poseidon, who *was* flooding. Hellenes believed deeply that the actions of their gods caused phenomena such as earthquakes, lightning, and floods.

To appease their gods, Hellenes built beautiful temples, sanctuaries, and altars whose ruins underlay and occasionally protrude up through the modern Grecian landscape. Temples to Artemis, Athena, Aphrodite, Dionysus, Apollo, and Demeter, among others, adorned Miletus from the eighth to the sixth century BC, until Persians razed them in the early fifth century BC. The fellow citizens of Heromotimus, celebrated prophet of Clazomenae, built a temple to honor him as a god after his wife burned his body while his soul was taking one of its occasional excursions to the remotest parts of the Earth to explain futurity to his countrymen.[42]

Caystrius, a son of Achilles and the Amazon Penthesileia—from whom the river Caystrus (Caystros) was believed to have derived—was, like Heromotimus, a hero to his countrymen, who honored him by building a sacred enclosure on the river Caystrus, which flowed near Ephesus.[43] A colossal temple (about 115 meters long and 55 meters wide) dedicated to Artemis at Ephesus (completed around 550 BC) was one of the Seven Wonders of the Ancient World designated by Herodotus. Ionians on Samos island built a huge temple to Hera at about the same time as the construction of the Artemis temple in Ephesus.

The relationship between the Hellenes and their gods was intense and nearly indestructible. Cumont writes about the Greek gods:

> The close resemblance of their [the gods'] feelings to those of their devotees [humans] leads them to mingle intimately in the earthly life of the latter; inspired by a like patriotism they take part with the opposing hosts in the strifes of the cities, of which they are the official protectors; they are the protagonists in all the causes which are espoused by their worshippers. These immortal beings, whose image has been impressed upon the world by an aristocratic epic, are but faintly distinguished from the warrior heroes who worship them, save by the radiance of eternal youth. And sculptors, by investing them with a sovereign grace and a serene majesty, enabled them to elevate and ravish the souls of men by the mere sight of their imperishable beauty. *The whole spirit of the Hellenic religion, profoundly human, ideally aesthetic, as poets and artists had fashioned it, was opposed to the deification of celestial bodies, far-off powers, devoid of feeling and of plastic form.*[44] [italics added]

In other words, the Greek multitude would prove unreceptive to the revolutionary cosmogonies, which were purposely devoid of feeling and emotion, as proposed by naturalist Ionian philosophers.

5. Ionian School of Philosophy

Ionia produced the first Greek philosophers in the sixth and fifth centuries BC. Thales (624–546 BC), Anaximander (610–546 BC), and Anaximenes (585–525 BC) lived in Miletus during the sixth century. A second group, which lived about a hundred years later, included Heraclitus of Ephesus (535–474 BC), Empedocles of Agrigentum, Sicily (490–430 BC), and Anaxagoras of Clazomenae (500–428 BC).

Greek biographer Sotion (200–170 BC) wrote the first known history to organize philosophers into schools of successive influence. He began his chronology with the "Ionian school," a subset of which was the "Milesian School" composed of Thales, Anaximander, and Anaximenes. There is "much justification for calling it a school in that all three men were natives of the same prosperous Ionian city of Miletus, their lifetimes overlapped, and tradition at least described their relations as those of master and pupil," notes Guthrie.[45] Anaxagoras and other later Ionian philosophers were members of the Ionian school, but not of the Milesian school.

Thales, Anaximander, and Anaximenes were the first "physicists," or students of nature, who sought natural explanations of the world without reference to supernatural beings. Hermann Diels' "Presocratic" moniker notwithstanding, Thales was the founder of Greek philosophy.[46] He said, for example, "[T]he world is held up by water and rides like a ship, and when it is said to 'quake' it is actually rocking because of the water's move-ment."[47] Thales' natural explanation struck at the heart of the Greeks' belief in Poseidon, Olympian god of the sea, who "commanded the respect, awe, and honour of all seafaring Greeks."[48] Poseidon was a violent god in a land wracked by earthquakes, which, along with flooding, were his signature handiwork. "Poseidon was not only worshipped, but feared. It is not surprising then, given this fear, that the Greeks were disturbed [when Thales suggested] that the fearful rumbling of the Earth was not controlled by the powerful Poseidon," notes Flem-Ath.[48]

Thales, Anaximander, and Anaximenes taught that "the world originated from a primitive substance, which was at once the matter out of which the world was made and the force by which the world was formed."[49] Thales identified the substance as water; Anaximander, as "the boundless"; and Anaximenes, as air or atmospheric vapor.[49] In addition, the three Milesian philosophers believed that *in* the primitive substance was "an inherent force, or vital power," thereby qualifying them as "hylozoists" and "dynamists," according to Turner.[50] *Hylozoism* is the belief that matter is alive. *Dynamism* is the belief that the original cosmothetic force was not distinct from, but identical to, the matter of the universe.[50-53] "It is impossible to determine whether these first philosophers were Theists or Pantheists, although one may perhaps infer from their hylozoistic cosmology that they believed 'God' to be at once the substance and the formative force in the university," notes Turner.[50]

Later Ionian philosophers (Heraclitus, Empedocles, Anaxagoras, and others) also were deeply interested in explaining the origin and nature of the universe. Unlike their predecessors, however, Heraclitus, Empedocles, and Anaxagoras tended to separate the primitive world-forming *force* from the primitive world-forming *matter*, though Heraclitus and Empedocles did so hesitatingly, using figurative language.[50, 54-55]

> Heraclitus was so impressed with the prevalence of change among physical things that he laid down the principle of pan-metabolism: *panta rei*, "all things are in a constant flux." Empedocles has the distinction of having introduced into philosophy the doctrine of four elements, or four "roots" as he calls them, namely, fire, air, earth, and water, out of which the centripetal force of love and the centrifugal force of hatred made all things, and are even now making and unmaking all things.[50]

Anaxagoras is notable for establishing clear boundaries between the cosmos-forming force (*Nous*) and original matter (that is, the primitive mixture). Aristotle, who later read Anaxagoras with great interest, noted that

Anaxagoras was the "first sober man" in a "crowd of random talkers who preceded him."[50]

Anaxagoras, like all Ionian philosophers, supplied *natural* causes for *observed phenomena* of the *physical world*, as did Thales with his theory of the natural cause of earthquakes. Anaxagoras had his own natural explanation for earthquakes: "The cosmic rotation causes the air under the earth to move. Sometimes the air gets caught up in the crevices of the earthy stuff. When this air cannot make its way out, the force of the moving air causes earthquakes."[56–57] Again, Anaxagoras makes plain that Poseidon was not a player in the realm of natural philosophy.

Ionian natural philosophers did not *invent* natural philosophy. Preliterate societies gleaned knowledge about the physical world from every kind of human pursuit, for example, hunting, sailing, and agriculture. However, Ionian philosophers were distinct from preliterate societies because they produced prose books using their native Ionian alphabet. Indeed, Ionian philosophers were the first known Western people to *write down* their theories about the physical world.

Durant notes that ten different Greek alphabets competed for ascendancy as an element of the wars of the Greek city-states. In Greece, the *Ionian form* prevailed. Ionian colonists transported it to Eastern Europe, where it survives today. The Romans adopted the *Chalcidian* or *Cumae form*, named after the towns of Chalcis and Cumae on the island of Euboea, the second-largest island in the Aegean Sea. The Chalcidian/Cumae alphabet became the Latin alphabet.[58]

The men who created the prose books using the Ionian alphabet "had as yet no name for themselves or their undertaking; at best they could designate themselves as wise, *sophoi* or *sophistai*," notes Burkert. "The term philosophy in its true sense was only coined by Plato," he adds. "As an expedient, the term Presocratics has won general acceptance, even if it is essentially negative," Burkert concludes.[59]

The natural systems of thought developed by Ionian philosophers lacked *teleology*. Derived from the Greek *telos* (meaning purpose or end), the term suggests that a purpose or directive principle exists in the works and processes of nature. According to Johansen, a teleologist would say, "the central task of cosmology [is] to articulate the way in which the cosmos manifests values, such as goodness and beauty."[60]

Socrates and Plato were ardent teleologists who admonished Anaxagoras for failing to apply the principle of teleology to his doctrine of worldforming *Nous*. Ionian philosophers, however, simply did not believe in "intelligent design" or other arguments for the existence of a creator that were based on perceived evidence of design, purpose, or direction in nature; their passion lay in explaining the physical world in nonemotional, nonsupernatural, and nonteleological terms.

6. Impact of Ionian Philosophy on Hellenic Religion

The rise of Ionian philosophy caused "change and revolution [to] finally … irrupt [*sic*] into the static structures of Greek religion," declares Burkert.[59] "It is tempting henceforth to dramatize intellectual history as a battle with successive attacks, victories, and defeats in which myth gradually succumbs to the *logos* and the archaic gives way to the modern," he notes. However, despite Burkert's assertions, most Hellenes continued to practice their beloved polytheistic religion while ridiculing—even prosecuting—the philosophers in their midst.

Mocking *testimonia* about Thales as the "typical philosopher" exist in Plato's *Theaetetus* (174a) and Aristotle's *Politics* (1259a9), respectively:

> A witty and attractive Thracian servant-girl is said to have mocked Thales for falling into a well while he was observing the stars and gazing upwards, declaring that he was eager to know the things in the sky, but that what was behind him and just by his feet escaped his notice.[61]

> When they reproached him [Thales] because philosophy [was useless], it is said that, having observed through his study of the heavenly bodies that there would be a large olive crop, he raised a little capital while it was still winter and paid deposits on all the olive presses in Miletus and Chios, hiring them cheaply because no one bid against him. When the appropriate time came, there was a sudden rush of requests for the presses. He then hired them out on his own terms and so made a large profit, thus demonstrating that it is easy for philosophers to be rich, if they wish, but that it is not in this that they are interested.[61]

Prosecution of philosophers as impious heretics landed Socrates, Anaxagoras, and Aristotle, among others, in Athenian courts. The Athenian multitude murdered the genial Socrates for his ideas; he had never physically harmed anyone.

If the Ionian philosophers did not transform the polytheistic religious landscape of Ionia in the sixth and fifth centuries BC, how did the philosophers change the world? Burkert's answer is that the philosophers verbalized new questions, developed new solutions, and *wrote down their ideas in books.*

> What does change as soon as philosophy appears on the scene is perspective and verbalization, the kind of questions asked. Previously, religion had been defined by forms of behavior and by institutions; now it becomes a matter of the theories and thoughts of individual men who express themselves in writing, in the form of books addressed to a nascent reading public. These are texts of a sort that did not exist before in either form or content: the new is incommensurable with the old. *Philosophy indeed begins with the prose book.*[59] [italics added]

The long-term impact of writing ideas onto manuscript pages cannot be overstated. Aristotle, for example, carefully studied Ionian ideas that had been earlier written on parchment and built his philosophy in part on them. In turn, his ideas, which he wrote down on parchment, in large part shaped the intellectual framework of the Middle Ages.

7. Anaxagoras of Clazomenae, Ionia

Anaxagoras was the son of Hegesibulus, or Eubulus, and a citizen of the Ionian city of Clazomenae, according to ancient biographer Diogenes Laertius.[62] Diogenes wrote:

> Anaxagoras was eminent for his noble birth and for his riches, and still more so for his magnanimity, inasmuch as he gave up all his patrimony to his relations; and being blamed … for his neglect of his estate "Why, then," said he, "do not you take care of it?" And at last, he abandoned it entirely, and devoted himself to the contemplation of subjects of natural philosophy, disregarding politics. So that once when some said to him "You have no affection for your country," "Be silent," said he, "for I have the greatest affection for my country," pointing up to heaven.[62]

As owner of a large estate in Clazemonae, Anaxagoras would likely have raised cereals, grapes, figs, and olives—that is, a lot of seed-based crops. He would have understood soil fertility and weather patterns as they related to the germination, growth, and harvesting of his seed crops. It is not unreasonable to suppose that Anaxagoras' knowledge of soils, seeds, and the weather would subsequently inform his natural philosophy.

8. *Anaxagoras in Athens, Attica*

Anaxagoras left Clazemonae to study philosophy in Athens at age twenty, during the archonship of Callias, according to Diogenes Laertius.[62] Sandywell surmises that upon his arrival in Athens in 480 BC, Anaxagoras probably created intense intellectual excitement as an ambassador of Ionian natural cosmology, which was still a rare and controversial import in Athens.[63] "For those who attended Anaxagoras' private lessons or who, like young Socrates, read his book, he was an authentic spokesman of the 'new science'—or what we would call today naturalistic inquiry. Anaxagoras was, for Socrates' generation, *the* natural philosopher and living connection with the great Ionian tradition of independent scientific inquiry," writes Sandywell.[63] Some of Anaxagoras' most famous pupils were Euripides, Pericles, Socrates, and Archelaus.[64]

By Diogenes Laertius' account, Anaxagoras touted his own ideas while in Athens.

> He asserted that the sun was a mass of burning iron, greater than Peloponnesus; ... and that the moon contained houses, and also hills and ravines: and that the primary elements of everything were similarities of parts; for as we say that gold consists of a quantity of grains combined together, so too is the universe formed of a number of small bodies of similar parts. He further taught that Mind [*Nous*] was the principle of motion: and that of bodies, the heavy ones, such as the earth, occupied the lower situations; and the light ones, such as fire, occupied the higher places, and that the middle spaces were assigned to water and air. And thus that the sea rested upon the earth, which was broad, the moisture being all evaporated by the sun. And he said that the stars originally moved about in irregular confusion, so that at first the pole star, which is continually visible, always appeared in the

zenith, but that afterwards it acquired a certain declination. And that the Milky Way was a reflection of the light of the sun when the stars did not appear. The comets he considered to be a concourse of planets emitting rays: and the shooting stars he thought were sparks as [if they] were leaping from the firmament. The winds he thought were caused by the rarification [*sic*] of the atmosphere, which was produced by the sun. Thunder, he said, was produced by the collision of the clouds; and lightning by the rubbing together of the clouds. Earthquakes, he said, were produced by the return of the air into the earth. All animals he considered were originally generated out of moisture, and heat, and earthy particles: and subsequently from one another. And males he considered were derived from those on the right hand, and females from those on the left.[62]

9. Aegospotami Meteorite

In 467 or 468 BC, a huge brown meteorite the size of a wagonload fell in broad daylight at Aegospotami (or Aegos Potami) near Sestos, Gallipoli Peninsula, which was in turn near the Hellespont, that is, the Dardanelles. The stone that fell from the sky confirmed Anaxagoras' astrophysical theory: *the heavenly bodies are stones, not gods.* Indeed, Anaxagoras had predicted that stones flying around in the cosmic vortex would occasionally dislodge and plummet to Earth.[65–67] People were able to visit the meteorite in the place that it fell as late as the time of Pliny (AD 23–79). Diogenes Laertius wrote:

> They say, also, that [Anaxagoras] predicted a fall of the stones which fell near Aegospotami, and which he said would fall from the sun: on which account Euripides, who was a disciple of his, said in his Phaethon that the sun was a golden clod of earth. He [Anaxagoras] went once to Olympia wrapped in a leathern cloak as if it were going to rain; and it did rain. And they say that he once replied to a man who asked him whether the mountains at Lampsacus would ever become sea, "Yes, if time lasts long enough."[62]

Anaxagoras visited the Aegospotami meteorite and was profoundly influenced by it. After years of observing the various heavenly bodies revolve overhead, Anaxagoras saw—and probably touched—one of them (or at least a piece of one), which others had actually witnessed falling to Earth. The large rock provided tangible and indisputable proof of his churning ideas about the cosmos. "[Anaxagoras] finally made up his mind to put his doctrine down in writing, publishing his book," which brought his ideas to a much wider and often unfriendly Athenian audience. His idea that "[t]he sun, the moon, and all the heavenly bodies are red-hot stones, which have been snatched up by the rotation of the aether," angered many Hellenes who were attached to their Olympian gods.[68]

10. Trial and Exile of Anaxagoras to Lampsacus

Anaxagoras was a close friend of Pericles (495–429 BC), the influential statesman, orator, and general of Athens during the city's Golden Age. Anaxagoras' natural philosophy contradicted the religious orthodoxy of the time. The two realities left him "vulnerable to those who wished to discredit the powerful and controversial student [Pericles] through the teacher [Anaxagoras]."[69]

At least two stories exist about how the Athenian justice system charged and tried Anaxagoras around 450 BC. According to Sotion's account, Cleon, a wealthy tanner and opponent of Pericles, charged Anaxagoras with impiety because he did not practice Cleon's polytheistic Greek religion and because he [Anaxagoras] claimed that the sun was a fiery lump and the moon was made of earth. An Athenian jury convicted Anaxagoras of impiety on the charge brought by Cleon, fined him five talents (a huge sum), and sent him into exile.[69]

By Satyrus' account, it was Thucydides, the son of Melesias and an enemy of Pericles, who accused Anaxagoras not only of impiety but also of Medism, that is, sympathy with the Medes, or Persians, whom the Hellenes loathed. (Medism was a crime in many Greek city-states, including Athens.)[69] An Athenian jury convicted Anaxagoras of impiety *and* Medism and condemned him to death *in absentia* (because Anaxagoras did not wait around for the verdict).[70] In either case, Anaxagoras appeared to suffer from his association with Pericles. Burnet suggests that Pericles helped Anaxagoras escape from prison and a sure Socrates-like fate.[70]

Driven from his adopted home, Anaxagoras returned to Ionia where he would be free to teach natural philosophy. As noted earlier, he settled at Lampsacus.[70] When Anaxagoras learned of his condemnation by the Athenian jury, he remarked, "Nature long ago condemned both them [the jury] and me." A man said to him, "You have lost the Athenians." Anaxagoras replied, "No, they have lost me."[62]

Anaxagoras organized a school in Lampsacus, and the people of Lampsacus embraced him as their fellow Ionian. Governors of Lampsacus granted his request that after his death (428 BC) the children would be allowed to play every year during the month in which he died.[62]

11. Anaxagoras' Cosmogony: Components and Process

The seven interlocking components of Anaxagoras' cosmogony are the primordial mixture, *Nous* (Mind), rotation, separation, multiple worlds, seeds, and conditions for growth.

A. Primordial Mixture

Anaxagoras proposed the existence of a primordial mixture made up of many kinds of "things." In this primordial mixture, "all things were together, unlimited both in amount and in smallness, for the small, too was unlimited. And because all things were together, nothing was evident on account of smallness; for air and aether covered everything, both being unlimited, for these are greatest among all things both in amount and in largeness."[71–72] By this, Anaxagoras meant that all things in the primordial mixture were so jumbled together and of such imperceptible size, particularly in contrast to the pervasive air and aether, which obscured everything, that an imaginary observer would see no distinction between each thing in the mix.[71]

The primordial mixture contained everything that was *real*. Thus, a combining of things in the mixture and a dissociation of things that had been mixed accounted for what human observers incorrectly believed were "coming to be" (birth) and "passing away" (death). Birth and death were only illusions, according to Anaxagoras. He asserted that what was really happening was association and disassociation of the primordial mixture, in Curd's words, "[mere] rearrangements" of the primordial mixture. Anaxagoras wrote, "The Greeks do not think correctly about "coming-to-be" (birth) and "passing-away" (death). For no thing comes to be or passes away, but is mixed together and dissociated from the things that are. And thus they would be right to call coming-to-be mixing-together and passing away dissociation."[73]

What are the "things" in the primordial mixture? A portion of the things is made up of seeds. About the seeds in the primordial mixture, Curd describes three scholarly accounts—the expansive, the austere, and the moderate views—full descriptions of which are beyond the scope of this monograph.[74] Note that the *seeds* about which Anaxagoras speaks in fragments B4a and B4b, discussed below, are *part of* the primordial mixture in all three accounts. The expansive view, according to Curd, posits three interpretations of the seeds, as

- "Biological starting points for plants and animals containing some of everything;
- Miniatures of each living thing that will or could develop throughout all time; or
- Very small fragments of each thing that is in the mixture."[75]

The idea of panspermia, as currently known and understood, views the Anaxagoras seeds as potential biological starting points for growth.

Cornford eloquently describes the primordial mixture as "the 'germ of the world,' analogous to the germ of the living creature and, for the same reason, as complex as the final product that emerges from it—the world with all its various parts and contents."[76]

B. *Nous* (Mind)

Anaxagoras proposed magnificent *Nous*, or Mind (or Intelligence or Force), in Fragment B12, in which he wrote, "The other things have a share of everything but *Nous* is unlimited and self-ruling and has been mixed with no thing, but is alone itself by itself."[77] Curd further describes *Nous* this way:

Nous is neither spatially limited nor limited in its powers ... There is no limit on the extent of *Nous* in the cosmos ... *Nous* is not governed or moved by anything except itself ... It alone makes decisions and moves things ... There is no level at which *Nous* could be part of any mixture ... The complete independence of *Nous* is summed up by the claim that it is "alone itself by itself," that is, it does not depend on anything else for its existence, either logically or causally.[78]

Anaxagoras wrote in Fragment B12: "It [*Nous*] is the finest of all things and the purest, and indeed it maintains all discernment about everything and has the greatest strength. And *Nous* has control over all things that have soul [or life], both the larger and the smaller."[77] Things with soul are "all living things (both plants and animals)," notes Curd.[79] She also argues that things with soul "would seem to qualify as things that have *Nous* in them."[77] Curd notes Sider's assertion that "living things share with *Nous* various degrees of cognitive, kinetic, and causal efficacy," and she continues, "This seems right, particularly if we add that living things are able to respond to their environments and, in some cases, reshape that environment."[79]

Anaxagoras' belief that *Nous* was distinct from the primordial mixture departed from the earlier Ionian philosophers, who did not distinguish as rigorously, if at all, between Mind (*Nous*) and matter (primordial mixture).

C. Rotation

Nous did something remarkable: it set the primordial mixture in revolving motion to form the cosmos. Anaxagoras wrote in Fragment B12, "*Nous* controlled the whole revolution, so that it started to revolve in the beginning. First, it began to revolve from a small region, but it is revolving yet more, and it will revolve still more."[78] The rotation (revolution) to which Anaxagoras referred is evident in the movement of heavenly bodies in the sky.

D. Separation

The speed and force of the rotation of the primordial mixture begun by *Nous* caused the different kinds of things in the primordial mixture to part swiftly. In Fragment B9, Anaxagoras explained, "[A]s these things are revolving in this way and being separated off by force and swiftness (the swiftness produces force), and their swiftness resembles the swiftness of nothing that is now present among humans, but is altogether many times as fast."[80]

The rotation produced a force capable of tearing apart the primordial mixture. If the rotation was ongoing, why did things appear more or less stable in the sky? The reason, replied Anaxagoras, was that the rotation that caused the initial and continuing separation (at the edges of the expanding rotation, as noted in Fragment B12) was a great deal faster than what was occurring in the region of the cosmos that people inhabited.[80]

Anaxagoras wrote (Fragment B12) that in the spinning of the primordial mixture through *Nous*, "the things being separated off now revolve, the stars and the sun and the moon and the air and the aether. This revolution caused them to separate off. The dense is being separated off from the rare, and the warm from the cold, and the bright from the dark, and the dry from the moist. But there are many shares of many things; nothing is completely separated off or dissociated one from the other except *Nous*."[81]

In Fragment B13, Anaxagoras wrote, "When *Nous* began to move [things], there was separation off from the multitude that was being moved, and whatever *Nous* moved, all this was dissociated; and as things were being moved and dissociated, the revolution made them dissociate much more."[81] He explained in Fragment B16, "From these, as they are being separated off, earth is compacted; for water is separated off from clouds, and earth from the water, and from the earth stones are compacted by the cold, and these stones move farther out than the water."[73]

E. Multiple Worlds

Anaxagoras specified in Fragment B4a that the rotation and separation occur both here and "elsewhere": "I have said this about the separation off, because there would be separation off not only for us but also elsewhere."[82] "These lines suggest that there are other worlds like our own in Anaxagoras' universe," argues Curd.[83]

> There have been a number of candidates for these other worlds: other places on our Earth, the moon, multiple parallel universes, worlds smaller than ours within our world. It has also been suggested that Anaxagoras is not committed to the reality of these worlds, but is merely engaging in thought experiment. *I [Curd] suggest that we take Anaxagoras seriously when he says that the rotation occurs not only here but elsewhere, and understand him to be saying that just as the rotation of the original mixture begun by Nous produces our world, so it will produce similar worlds in other areas of the rotation* [italics added]. The passage (B4a) begins by saying what must be the case given certain initial conditions; it goes on to explain that the mechanism of rotation will have similar results everywhere because the mix of the original ingredients will behave in the same way as the rotation spreads out through the indefinitely extended mass of ingredients.[83]

Cornford concurs with Curd, Burnet, and others: Anaxagoras meant that "there [were] other, and indeed innumerable, worlds besides our own."[84–85]

F. Seeds

The primordial mixture comprises all kinds of things, including Anaxagoras' famous seeds. Anaxagoras mentioned seeds only twice in the extant fragments (Fragment B4a and Fragment B4b), as follows:

> Fragment B4a: Since these things are so, it is right to think that there are many different things present in everything that is being combined, and *seeds* [emphasis added] of all things, having all sorts of forms, colours, and flavours.[86]

> Fragment B4b: Before there was separation off, because all things were together, there was not even any colour evident; for the mixture of all things prevented it, of the wet and the dry and of the hot and the cold

and of the bright and the dark, and there was much earth present and *seeds* unlimited in number, in no way similar to one another. For no one of the others is similar to another.[87]

What does Anaxagoras mean by the term *seeds*? Schofield answers: "There are few more contentious issues in the interpretation of Anaxagoras than the identity of his seeds."[88] Curd argues that the things in the primordial mixture "will produce stuffs and the natural features of the world such as rocks, mountains, rivers, and stars, but Anaxagoras may have felt the need to explain structured living things as well."[89] She continues, "The seeds deal with that problem. The seeds are growth points for living things, and contain all the ingredients for the beginning of an organism, in addition to, perhaps, some sort of structural aspect (probably directed by *Nous*)."[89]

Returning briefly to Fragment B4a, important text bearing on the identity of seeds follows "forms, colours, and flavours":

> Fragment B4a: Since these things are so, it is right to think that there are many different things present in everything that is being combined, and seeds of all things, having all sorts of forms, colours, and flavours, *that humans and also the other animals were compounded, as many as have soul. Also that there are cities that have been constructed by humans and works made, just as with us, and that there are a sun and a moon and other heavenly bodies for them, just as with us, and the earth grows many different things for them, the most valuable of which they gather together into their household and use.*[82] [italics added]

Cornford interprets the meaning of the italicized passage above, as follows:

> Any ordinary Greek, reading this passage … would take "seeds" to mean the seeds of plants and animals; and any doubt about this would be removed by the next statement, that men and all other living creatures were formed [compounded]; they grew, he would suppose, from the seeds just mentioned.[90]

Furthermore, the addition of the final sentence of Fragment B4a ["I [Anaxagoras] have said this about the separation off, because there would be separation off not only for us but also everywhere"] suggests "the whole paragraph … naturally convey[s] that life has arisen from seeds independently in other parts of the world [universe] as well as in ours," avers Cornford. *This is the core belief of panspermia*, that "seeds" in the universe infall to Earth and other celestial bodies to yield "life" when conditions are ripe (see "Conditions for Growth" below).

Vlastos points out that Anaxagoras was the first philosopher to introduce the term *seeds* into the technical vocabulary of Greek cosmogony. His "other technical terms—mixture, segregation, composition, and the rest—are strikingly traditional," declares Vlastos. "But *no one before Anaxagoras had ever used 'seed' as he did, while after him the term became current in physical terminology.*"[91] [italics added] Perhaps Ionian seeds—barley, wheat, millet, grapes, olives, figs, and lentils—remained alive in his mind as he toiled in the urban chaos of Athens.

For those scholars who would interpret seeds in a variety of arcane ways, Cornford argues persuasively for allowing Anaxagoras' word *seed* "to carry its normal force," that is, seeds are growth points for propagation of plants and animals. Schofield agrees with Cornford's argument.[92]

G. Conditions for Growth

Anaxagoras said nothing in the extant fragments about any "conditions" that may be necessary for a seed to sprout once it has reached a celestial body. There are subsequent *testimonia*, however, that address this point. Theophrastus was a zoologist, among other things, and was the successor to Aristotle in the latter's Lyceum school in Athens. According to the Theophrastan tradition, "animals originally came to be in the wet, but afterwards from each other." Diogenes Laertius asserted, "Animals came to be from the wet and hot and earthy, but later from each other." Theophrastus also wrote, "Anaxagoras says that the air contains seeds of all things and that these, when carried down with water, generate plants."[93]

(Note that this Theophrastan passage is *testimonia*, not *ipsissima verba*, exact words of the author.)

Schofield summarizes the necessity for conditions to be ripe for growth once seeds have landed on a celestial body:

> Just as the seeds of plants can exist in the air independently of any parent body, and begin to grow in the wet earth, so ([Anaxagoras] probably reasoned) the seeds of animals existed in the air and aither [ether] which covered the primordial mixture, again independently of any parent body, and began to grow once they had found a home in the warm, wet earth that became concentrated at the centre of the cosmic rotation [Anaxagoras believed that the Earth was the center of the universe]. Such a possibility makes good Anaxagorean sense, so long as we suppose that he recognized normal plant reproduction, too. For if more air and aither are always being separated off by the cosmic rotation, one would expect seeds to be separated off with them.[93]

The point here is that the crucial materials necessary for the emergence of plant and animal life are threefold: seeds (the "stuff and organizing principle of life"), Earth (or other worlds, the essential nursery), and the ability for animals and plants to reproduce on Earth (or other worlds).[94] Anaxagoras' seeds of life spin out of the cosmic vortex begun by *Nous*, to infall to Earth and other celestial bodies; to wit, the theory of panspermia.

12. Summary

Anaxagoras of Clazomenae was a wealthy Ionian landowner, farmer, and natural philosopher in the fifth century BC whose cosmogony is the first known written articulation of the theory of panspermia. His theory contradicted his contemporaries' beliefs about the origin of the cosmos. Elements of his cosmogony include *Nous*, primordial mixture, rotation, separation, multiple worlds, seeds, and conditions for growth. Anaxagoras was the first philosopher to use the term *seed* in his cosmogony. In a continuous and ongoing process, *Nous* set the primordial mixture into swift and forceful rotation that separated seeds out of the mixture, causing them to fall to Earth and other worlds where they propagated into living things when conditions were ripe.

Anaxagoras' cosmogony suffered at the hands of Plato, who denigrated it and Aristotle, who misinterpreted it.[95] However, Anaxagoras' cosmogony, including the theory of panspermia, has survived and evolved to the present time as the scientific discipline of astrobiology, "the study of life as a planetary phenomenon."[96]

Notes

1. Anaxagoras scholar Felix M. Cleve notes "no less than three different versions" of "the dates of the main items in Anaxagoras' biography." Felix M. Cleve, *The Philosophy of Anaxagoras* (King's Crown Press, 1949), ix–x. Cleves writes:

> Version Number One. Anaxagoras was born in Klazomenae in 500 BC, lived and taught in Athens from 461 to 432, was accused and sentenced to death in 432, and having been rescued by his *friend* [italics by Cleve] Pericles, left for Lampsakos, where he died in 428. This is the current, "orthodox" version, based on Apollodorus' somewhat schematic statements and backed by authorities like Diels; which is to say that it is accepted by the majority. [Hermann Diels searched Greek literature for actual quotations from Presocratic authors. In 1903, he published *Die Fragmente der Vorsokratiker* (The Fragments of the Presocratics).] Version Number Two. Lifetime: 500–428, as above; residence in Athens: 480–450; date of the trial: 450; then residence in Lampsakos, where he conducts a flourishing and influential school of philosophy for the last two decades of his life. This version was 'established' by A. E. Taylor in a clever essay, *"On the Date of the Trial of Anaxagoras,"*—supported by a number of quite impressive arguments. Version Number Three. Anaxagoras was born in—533, came to Athens in 494 (after the fall of Miletus), and taught there for thirty years. His most famous pupils were Themistocles, Pericles, and Euripides. After the fall of the meteoric stone of Aigospotamoi [*sic*] in 467/6, which confirmed his astrophysical theories, he finally made up his mind to put his doctrine down in writing, published his book in 466 and, thereupon, was indicted and sentenced to death "for impiety and Persian leanings" in 465.

Rescued by his *pupil* [italics by Cleve] Pericles, who was just successfully beginning his career at that time, he left for Lampsakos (then still under Persian rule), where he died some years later, 462 or 461. This version was established in 1884 by Georg Friedrich Unger in a brilliant, detailed research on "Die Zeitverhaltnisse des Anaxagoras und Empdokles," in which he accounts for all his statements with really convincing reasons. I [Cleve] quote only one of these arguments: Aside from the fact that in none of the Platonic dialogues is Anaxagoras introduced as a living person, Socrates, who was born in 468, attended lectures by Archelaos, a disciple of Anaxagoras; would he have done so if Anaxagoras himself had been available as a lecturer in Athens until 423? ... There are then, no less than three sets of 'established facts,' differing greatly from each other. You can make your own choice.

Which version did Cleve support? He preferred version number three, "[n]ot merely because Diels, who later became *Geheimrat* [a very eminent professor in some universities] in Berlin, had the power to silence Unger, who had dared to disagree, but, above all, for internal reasons."

2. Neuter gender is a grammatical gender that includes *those nouns having referents that do not have distinctions of sex*. Source: "What is neuter gender?" http://www.sil.org/linguistics/GlossaryOfLinguisticTerms/WhatIsNeuterGender.htm (accessed January 20, 2008). See also N. N. Zabinkova, "Generic Names Ending in -ma and Family Names Derived from Them," *Taxon* 14, no. 6 (July 1965): 184–187. Zabinkova notes, "*Greek* [italics added] nouns ending in -*ma* are neuter and their stem includes the final element -*at*-, e.g., 'sperma,' 'spermatos' (seed), 'derma,' 'dermatos' (skin), 'nema,' 'nematos' (thread), 'stigma,' 'stigmatos' (tattoo-mark, spot), and so on. As a rule the words derived from them retain the element -*at*-; e.g., 'spermaticos' (of seed, seminal), 'dermaticos' (of skin), etc., though sometimes the derived words have a somewhat changed stem; thus Hippocrates used the word 'epidermis,' 'epidermidos' (outer skin) which, though having a common origin with the word 'derma', does not retain the stem *dermat*—in full

... In *classical Latin* [emphasis added] there are nouns ending in *-ma* of both Greek and Latin origin. Latin words such as 'forma' (form), 'lacrima' (tear), 'struma' (a scrofulous tumour) are feminine and their stem does not end in *-at-*. Nouns of *Greek* origin ending in *-ma* retain in *Latin* [emphasis added] their neuter gender and their stem; they are declined as Latin words of the III declension ... e.g., 'nema,' nematis' (threat), 'sperma', 'spermatis' (seed), and many others." (See page 185.)

3.   Richard Lattimore, *The Iliad of Homer* (Chicago: University of Chicago Press, 1951), 497. John Chadwick, *The Decipherment of Linear B* (Cambridge, UK: Cambridge University Press, 2003), 104.

4.   U.S. National Aeronautics and Space Administration, "Astrobiology," http://astrobiology.arc.nasa.gov/ (accessed February 1, 2008).

5.   Arthur Fairbanks, *The First Philosophers of Greece: An Edition and Translation of the Remaining Fragments of the Pre-Sokratic Philosophers* (London: Kegan Paul, Trench, Trubner & Co., 1898), v–vii.

6.   Simplicius (AD 490–560) was born in Cilicia in southern Anatolia and studied Aristotle and Plato in Athens with Neoplatonist philosopher Damascius, the last head of Plato's Academy when the Christian emperor Justinian closed it in AD 529. Simplicius was one of the most important sources for the Ionian philosophers. Many fragments of Anaxagoras are preserved only in Simplicius' works. Simplicius wrote commentaries that "did not overestimate his own contributions" as he "was aware of his debt to other philosophers." He "carefully constructed interpretations of the writings of Aristotle and attempted to harmonize the views of Plato and Aristotle." J. J. O'Connor and E. F. Robertson, "Simplicius," http://www-groups.dcs.st-and.ac. uk/~history/Biographies/Simplicius.html (accessed January 30, 2008). Ilsetraut Hadot, "The Life and Work of Simplicius in Greek and Arabic Sources," in *Aristotle Transformed: The Ancient Commentators and Their Influence*, ed. Richard Sorabji (Ithaca, NY: Cornell University Press, 1990), 275–304.

7. Simplicius, *Simplicius on Aristotle's Physics* (Ithaca, NY: Cornell University Press, 1997).

8. Sextus Empiricus (AD 160–210) was a Greek physician and philosopher as well as a pupil and successor of the medical skeptic Herodotus (not the historian) of Tarsus. Empiricus probably lived in Rome, Alexandria, and Athens. His work is a valuable source for the history of thought, especially because of his development and formulation of former skeptic doctrines. (*Skeptic* derives from the Greek verb *skeptesthai*, meaning to examine closely.) http://plato.stanford.edu/entries/skepticism-ancient/ (accessed January 30, 2008). R. G. Bury, *Outlines of Pyrrhonism: Sextus Empiricus*, Great Books in Philosophy (Buffalo, NY: Prometheus Books, 1990).

9. Hermann Diels and Walther Kranz, eds. *Die Fragmente der Vorsokratiker* (Berlin: Wiedmann, 1985).

10. "Hanover Historical Texts Project," http://history.hanover.edu/project.html#20 (accessed February 10, 2008). Scroll down to "Ancient Greece and Rome." Each of the links (for example, Anaxagoras, Anaximander, and Anaximenes) corresponds to a chapter of Fairbanks' book, *The First Philosophers of Greece*.

11. "Diels-Kranz Numbering System," *The Internet Encyclopedia of Philosophy*, http://www.iep.utm.edu/ancillaries/dk.htm (accessed January 31, 2008).

12. Kathleen Freeman, *Ancilla to the Pre-Socratic Philosophers* (Cambridge, MA: Harvard University Press, 2003). This book is a complete English translation of the *B* passages—the so-called fragments from *Die Fragmente der Vorsokratiker*. The ancilla for Anaxagoras are located on pages 82–85 in the 2003 edition of *Ancilla*.

13. Patricia Curd, *Anaxagoras of Clazomenae: Fragments and Testimonia (Phoenix Presocratic Series)* (Toronto: University of Tor-

onto Press, 2007), 1–2. Curd presents the fragments in their contexts on pages 14–29.

14. Felix M. Cleve, *The Philosophy of Anaxagoras* (New York: King's Crown Press, Columbia University, 1949).

15. F. M. Cornford, "Anaxagoras' theory of matter," in *Studies in Presocratic Philosophy. International Library of Philosophy and Scientific Method*, vol. 2, *Eleatics and Pluralists*, R. E. Allen and David J. Furley, eds. (Humanities Press, 1975).

16. Patricia Curd, *Anaxagoras of Clazomenae: Fragments and Testimonia (Phoenix Presocratic Series)* (Toronto: University of Toronto Press, 2007).

17. Malcolm Schofield, *An Essay on Anaxagoras,* Cambridge Classical Studies (Cambridge, UK: Cambridge University Press, 1980).

18. David Sider, *The Fragments of Anaxagoras*, 2nd ed. (Sankt Augustin, Germany: Academic Verlag, 2005). See http://www.academiaverlag.de/titel/69293.htm for purchase (accessed February 2, 2008).

19. Gregory Vlastos, "One world or many in Anaxagoras?" in *Studies in Presocratic Philosophy. International Library of Philosophy and Scientific Method*, vol. 2, *Eleatics and Pluralists*. R. E. Allen and David J. Furley, eds. (Atlantic Highlands, NJ: Humanities Press, 1975), 354–360.

20. Felix M. Cleve, *The Philosophy of Anaxagoras* (New York: King's Crown Press, Columbia University, 1949), viii. Italics in the quote are by Cleve.

21. R. M. Cook and Pierre DuPont, *East Greek Pottery,* Readings in Classical Archaeology (London: Routledge, 1998), 1–5.

22. Ibid., 1.

23. The term Asia Minor was not used until the fifth century AD. The name Anatolia was first used in the tenth century AD. Freya Stark, *Ionia: A Quest* (New York: Harcourt, Brace and Company, 1954), 229.

24. Vanessa B. Gorman, *Miletos: The Ornament of Ionia: A History of the City to 400 BCE* (Ann Arbor, MI: University of Michigan Press, 2001).

25. Alan M. Greaves, *Miletos: A History* (London: Routledge, 2002).

26. Herodotus, *The Histories,* Book I:142 (London: Penguin Classics, 2003), 65.

27. Freya Stark, *Ionia: A Quest* (New York: Harcourt, Brace and Company, 1954), 17–18.

28. Vanessa B. Gorman, *Miletos: The Ornament of Ionia: A History of the City to 400 BCE* (Ann Arbor, MI: University of Michigan Press, 2001), 125.

29. Ibid., 129–163.

30. R. M. Cook and Pierre DuPont, *East Greek Pottery*, Readings in Classical Archaeology (London: Routledge, 1998), 3.

31. Herodotus, *The Histories,* Book I:148 (London: Penguin Classics, 2003), 67.

32. R. M. Cook and Pierre DuPont, *East Greek Pottery,* Readings in Classical Archaeology (London: Routledge, 1998), 4.

33. James Pillans, *Elements of Physical and Classical Geography* (Edinburgh: William Blackwood & Sons, 1854), 92–93.

34. Alan M. Greaves, *Miletos: A History* (London: Routledge, 2002), 9, 20, 24–25, 29, 30, 32, 101–102.

35. Deborah N. Carlson, "Classical Greek Shipwreck: Tektas Burnu, Turkey," *American Journal of Archaeology* 107, no. 4 (October 2003): 581–600, http://www.ajaonline.org/pdfs/107.4/AJA1074.pdf#carlson (accessed January 30, 2008).

36. Vanessa B. Gorman, *Miletos: The Ornament of Ionia: A History of the City to 400 BCE* (Ann Arbor, MI: University of Michigan, 2001), 60.

37. Will Durant, *The Life of Greece* (New York: Simon and Schuster, 1939), 134–135.

38. Vanessa B. Gorman, *Miletos: The Ornament of Ionia: A History of the City to 400 BCE* (Ann Arbor, MI: University of Michigan, 2001), 243–245. John Burnet, *Early Greek Philosophy* (Whitefish, MT: Kessinger Publishing, 2003), 256.

39. Thomas Bulfinch, *Bulfinch's Mythology* (New York: Modern Library, 1998). Edith Hamilton, *Mythology* (New York: Back Bay Books, 1998). Martin P. Nilsson, *The Mycenaean Origin of Greek Mythology* (Berkeley: University of California Press, 1972).

40. Mary Settegast, *Plato Prehistorian: 10,000 to 5,000 BC* (Hudson, NY: Lindisfarne Press, 1990). W. K. C. Guthrie, *The Greeks and Their Gods* (Boston: Beacon Press, 1971).

41. Richard Lattimore, *The Iliad of Homer* (Chicago: University of Chicago Press, 1951), 54.

42. John Bell, *Bell's New Pantheon or Historical Dictionary of the Gods, Demi Gods, Heroes and Fabulous Personages of Antiquity* (Whitefish, MT: Kessinger Publishing, 2003), 395.

43. Ibid., 162. See also "Caystrius," *Greek Myth Index*, http://mythindex.com/greek-mythology/C/Caystrius.html (accessed January 28, 2008).

44. Franz Cumont, *Astrology and Religion among the Greeks and Romans* (New York: Cosimo Classics, 2006), 23.

45. W. K. C. Guthrie, *Greek Philosophers: From Thales to Aristotle* (New York: Harper Perennial, 1960), 23.

46. Arthur Fairbanks, *The First Philosophers of Greece: An Edition and Translation of the Remaining Fragments of the Pre-Sokratic Philosophers* (London: Kegan Paul, Trench, Trubner & Co., 1898), 1.

47. Geoffrey Stephen Kirk and John Earle Raven, *Presocratic Philosophers* (Cambridge, UK: Cambridge University Press, 1984), 93.

48. Rand Flem-Ath, *When the Sky Fell: In Search of Atlantis* (New York: St. Martin's Paperbacks, 1997), 138.

49. Arthur Fairbanks, *The First Philosophers of Greece: An Edition and Translation of the Remaining Fragments of the Pre-Sokratic Philosophers* (London: Kegan Paul, Trench, Trubner & Co., 1898) (See page 1 for Thales, page 11 for Anaxamandros, and page 21 for Anaximenes).

50. William Turner, "Ionian School of Philosophy," transcribed by Tomas Hancil, in *The Catholic Encyclopedia*, vol. 3 (New York: Robert Appleton Company, 1910). http://www.newadvent.org/cathen/08092a.htm (accessed January 26, 2008).

51. For more information on hylozoists and dynamists, see William Turner, "Hylozoism," transcribed by Tomas Hancil, in *The Catholic Encyclopedia*, vol. 7 (New York: Robert Appleton Company, 1910). http://www.newadvent.org/cathen/07594a.htm (accessed January 28, 2008). See also William Turner, "Dynamism," transcribed by Douglas J. Potter, in *The Catholic Encyclopedia*, vol. 5 (New York: Robert Appleton Company, 1909). http://www.newadvent.org/cathen/05222a.htm (accessed January 28, 2008).

52. *Hylozoism* is "the view that all matter is alive." Donald M. McKim, *Westminster Dictionary of Theological Terms* (Louisville, KY: Westminster John Knox Press, 1996), 135.

53. *Cosmothetic* pertains to a doctrine that affirms the real existence of the external world. *Webster's International Dictionary,* 2nd ed. (Springfield, MA: G.C. Merriam Company, 1941), 601.

54. Some fragments of Heraclitus' writing survive and are available in T. M. Robinson, *Heraclitus* (Toronto: University of Toronto Press, 1987). For an example of a discussion of matter, see page 99.

55. Arthur Fairbanks, ed. and trans. "Empedocles Fragments and Commentary," in *The First Philosophers of Greece* (London: Kegan Paul, Trench, Trubner & Co. 1898), 157–234, http://history.hanover.edu/texts/presoc/emp.htm (accessed January 28, 2008).

56. "Anaxagoras," *Stanford Encyclopedia of Philosophy,* August 22, 2007, http://plato.stanford.edu/entries/anaxagoras/#MetGeo (accessed January 17, 2008).

57. William Herbert Hobbs, *Earthquakes: An Introduction to Seismic Geology* (New York: D. Appleton and Company, 1907), 7–8.

58. Durant notes the oldest Greek inscriptions, dating from the seventh and sixth centuries BC, show a close resemblance to the Semitic characters on the ninth-century Moabite stone, bearing a thirty-four-line inscription written by the Moabite king Mesha (first discovered in 1868). The Greeks added vowels to the Semitic words. (The Semites used characters denoting consonants or breathing to represent *a, e, i, o,* and *u.*) Later the Ionians added the long vowels *eta* (long *e*) and *omega* (long or double *o*). Will Durant, *The Life of Greece* (New York: Simon and Schuster, 1939), 205.

59. Walter Burkert, *Greek Religion: Archaic and Classical,* Ancient World (Cambridge, MA: Harvard University Press, 2006), 305–306.

60. Thomas Kjeller Johansen, *Plato's Natural Philosophy: A Study of the Timaeus-Critias* (Cambridge, UK: Cambridge University Press, 2004), 1–3.

61. Plato, *Theaetetus* (Newburyport, MA: Focus Publishing, 2004), 64. Aristotle, *Politics* (London: Penguin Classics, 1981), 90.

62. Diogenes Laertius, "Life of Anaxagoras," trans. C. D. Yonge, in *Lives and Opinions of Eminent Philosophers,* http://www.classicpersuasion.org/pw/diogenes/dlanaxagoras.htm (accessed January 29, 2008).

63. Barry Sandywell, *Presocratic Reflexivity: The Construction of Philosophical Discourse 600–450 BC: Logological Investigations,* vol. 3 (London: Routledge, 1996), 366.

64. Thucydides provides these names (except Archelaus) as Anaxagoras' most famous students in Thucydides, *The History of the Peloponnesian War,* trans. William Smith (New York: Harper & Brothers, 1855), xxv.

65. E. Theodossious, P. G. Niarchos, V. N. Manimanis, W. Orchiston, "The Fall of a Meteorite at Aegos Potami in 467/6 BC," *Journal of Astronomical History and Heritage* 5, no. 2 (2002), 135–140.

66. Anthony Preus, *Notes on Greek Philosophy from Thales to Aristotle* (Newport Pagnell, UK: Global Publications, 1997), 20.

67. Massimo D'Orazio, "Meteorite Records in the Ancient Greek and Latin Literature: Between History and Myth," *Myth and Geology,* vol. 273, ed. L. Piccardi and W. B. Masse (London: Geological Society of London, 2007), 216–217.

68. "Anaxagoras," *The Internet Encyclopedia of Philosophy,* http://www.iep.utm.edu/a/anaxagor.htm (accessed January 31, 2008).

69. Jonathan Barnes, *Early Greek Philosophy* (London: Penguin, 2002), 187.

70. John Burnet, *Early Greek Philosophy* (Whitefish, MT: Kessinger Publishing, 2003), 256.

71. Aristotle thought that Anaxagoras' "all things together" primary mixture was such an important concept, he placed it at (or near) the opening of book 1 of *Physics*, according to Simplicius. Patricia Curd, *Anaxagoras of Clazomenae: Fragments and Testimonia,* Phoenix Presocratic Series (Toronto: University of Toronto Press, 2007), 153.

72. Anaxagoras Fragment B1. Ibid., 15, 33–36.

73. Anaxagoras Fragment B17. Ibid., 27, 72–73.

74. Patricia Curd, *Anaxagoras of Clazomenae: Fragments and Testimonia,* Phoenix Presocratic Series (Toronto: University of Toronto Press, 2007) 154–171.

75. Ibid., 157.

76. F. M. Cornford, "Anaxagoras' Theory of Matter," in *Studies in Presocratic Philosophy.* vol. 2, *Eleatics and Pluralists,* ed. R. E. Allen and David J. Furley (Atlantic Highlands, NJ: Humanities Press, 1975), 286–287.

77. Anaxagoras Fragment B12. Patricia Curd, *Anaxagoras of Clazomenae: Fragments and Testimonia,* Phoenix Presocratic Series (Toronto: University of Toronto Press, 2007), 23–24, 66–67.

78. Patricia Curd, *Anaxagoras of Clazomenae: Fragments and Testimonia,* Phoenix Presocratic Series (University of Toronto Press, 2007), 56.

79. Ibid., 61.

80. Ibid., 52.

81. Ibid., 25.

82. Ibid., 42.

83. Ibid., 45.

84. John Burnet, *Early Greek Philosophy*, 3rd ed., (London: Adam and Charles Black, 1920), 272–300, http://www.classicpersuasion.org/pw/burnet/egp.htm?chapter=6#N_34_ (accessed January 13, 2008).

85. F. M. Cornford, "Innumerable Worlds in Presocratic Philosophy," *The Classical Quarterly* 28, no. 1 (January 1934), 7. Gregory Vlastos, "One World or Many in Anaxagoras?" in *Studies in Presocratic Philosophy*. vol. 2, *Eleatics and Pluralists*, eds. R. E. Allen and David J. Furley, (Atlantic Highlands, NJ: Humanities Press, 1975), 354–360.

86. Patricia Curd, *Anaxagoras of Clazomenae: Fragments and Testimonia*, Phoenix Presocratic Series (Toronto: University of Toronto Press, 2007), 16–17, 42–45.

87. Ibid., 18–19, 45–47.

88. Malcolm Schofield, *An Essay on Anaxagoras*, Cambridge Classical Studies (Cambridge, UK: Cambridge University Press, 1980), 106.

89. Patricia Curd, *Anaxagoras of Clazomenae: Fragments and Testimonia*, Phoenix Presocratic Series (Toronto: University of Toronto Press, 2007), 43–44.

90. F. M. Cornford, "Innumerable Worlds in Presocratic Philosophy," *The Classical Quarterly* 28, no. 1 (January 1934), 8.

91. Vlastos, Gregory, "The Physical Theory of Anaxagoras" *Philosophical Review* 59 (1950), 31–57, in *Studies in Presocratic Philosophy*. *International Library of Philosophy and Scientific Method*, vol. 2, *Eleatics and Pluralists*, Allen, R. E. and David J. Furley, eds., Atlantic Highlands, NJ: Humanities Press, 1975, 323–353.

92. Malcolm Schofield, *An Essay on Anaxagoras*, Cambridge Classical Studies (Cambridge, UK: Cambridge University Press, 1980), 164, n. 41.

93. Ibid., 124–125.

94. Ibid., 126.

95. Margaret R. O'Leary, *Plato and the Panspermia Controversy* (iUniverse, Inc., forthcoming).

96. Lucas J. Mix, "Astrobiology Primer: An Outline of General Knowledge—Version 1, 2006," *Astrobiology* vol. 6, no. 5 (2006): 739, http://www.liebertonline.com/doi/pdfplus/10.1089/ast.2006.6.735?cookieSet=1 (accessed February 9, 2008).

Select Bibliography

Allen, Reginald E. *Greek Philosophy: Thales to Aristotle,* Readings in the History of Philosophy. New York: Free Press, 1991.

Allen, R. E. and David J. Furley, eds. *Studies in Presocratic Philosophy. International Library of Philosophy and Scientific Method,* vol. 2, *Eleatics and Pluralists,* (Atlantic Highlands, NJ: Humanities Press, 1975).

"Anaxagoras." *The Internet Encyclopedia of Philosophy.* http://www.iep.utm.edu/a/anaxagor.htm (accessed January 31, 2008).

"Anaxagoras." *Stanford Encyclopedia of Philosophy.* August 2007. http://plato.stanford.edu/entries/anaxagoras/ (accessed February 5, 2008).

Aristotle. *The Politics of Aristotle.* Chapel Hill, NC: University of North Carolina Press, 1997.

Aristotle. *The Treatises of Aristotle: On the Heavens, On Generation and Corruption and On Meteors.* Boston: Adamant Media Corporation, 2006.

Bakewell, Charles M. *Sourcebook in Ancient Philosophy.* New York: Charles Scribner's Sons, 1907.

Barnes, Jonathan, *Early Greek Philosophy.* London: Penguin, 2002.

Bell, John. *Bell's New Pantheon or Historical Dictionary of the Gods, Demi Gods, Heroes and Fabulous Personages of Antiquity.* Whitefish, MT: Kessinger Publishing, 2003.

Bulfinch, Thomas. *Bulfinch's Mythology.* New York: Modern Library, 1998.

Burkert, Walter. *Greek Religion: Archaic and Classical,* Ancient World. Cambridge, MA: Harvard University Press, 2006.

Burnet, John. *Early Greek Philosophy.* Whitefish, MT: Kessinger Publishing, 2003.

Bury, J. B. *A History of Greece to the Death of Alexander the Great.* New York: Palgrave Macmillan, 2000.

Bury, R. G. *Outlines of Pyrrhonism: Sextus Empiricus,* Great Books in Philosophy. Buffalo, NY: Prometheus Books, 1990.

Carlson, Deborah N. "Classical Greek Shipwreck: Tektas Burnu, Turkey." *American Journal of Archaeology* 107, no. 4 (October 2003): 581–600. http://www.ajaonline.org/pdfs/107.4/AJA1074.pdf#carlson. (accessed January 30, 2008).

Cleve, Felix M. *The Philosophy of Anaxagoras.* New York: King's Crown Press, Columbia University, 1949.

Cook, R. M. and Pierre DuPont, *East Greek Pottery,* Readings in Classical Archaeology. London: Routledge, 1998.

Cornford, F. M., "Anaxagoras' Theory of Matter," *The Classical Quarterly* 28, no. 1 (January 1934), 8, in *Studies in Presocratic Philosophy. International Library of Philosophy and Scientific Method,* vol. 2, *Eleatics and Pluralists,* Allen, R. E. and David J. Furley, eds., Atlantic Highlands, NJ: Humanities Press, 1975, 275–322.

Cornford, F. M. "Innumerable Worlds in Presocratic Philosophy." *The Classical Quarterly* 28, no. 1 (January 1934): 1–16.

Cumont, Franz. *Astrology and Religion among the Greeks and Romans.* 1912. New York: Cosimo Classics, 2006.

Curd, Patricia. *Anaxagoras of Clazomenae: Fragments and Testimonia,* Phoenix Presocratic Series. Toronto: University of Toronto Press, 2007.

Davison, J. A. "Protagoras, Democritus, and Anaxagoras." *The Classical Quarterly* 3, no. 1/2 (January–April 1953): 33–45.

Diels, Hermann and Walther Kranz, eds. *Die Fragmente der Vorsokratiker.* Berlin: Wiedmann, 1985.

Diogenes Laertius. "Life of Anaxagoras." Translated C. D. Yonge. *Lives and Opinions of Eminent Philosophers.* http://www. classicpersuasion.org/pw/diogenes/dlanaxagoras.htm (accessed January 29, 2008).

D'Orazio, Massimo. "Meteorite Records in the Ancient Greek and Latin Literature: Between History and Myth." In *Myth and Geology* 273, edited by L. Piccardi and W. B. Masse, 216–217. London: Geological Society of London, 2007.

Durant, Will. *The Life of Greece.* New York: Simon and Schuster, 1939.

Durant, Will. *The Story of Philosophy.* New York: Pocket Books, 1961.

Fairbanks, Arthur, ed. and trans. "Anaxagoras' Fragments and Commentary." In *The First Philosophers of Greece*, 235–262. London: Kegan Paul, Trench, Trubner & Co. 1898. http://history.hanover.edu/ texts/presoc/anaxagor.htm (accessed February 2, 2008).

Fairbanks, Arthur, ed. and trans. "Empedocles Fragments and Commentary." In *The First Philosophers of Greece*, 157–234. London: Kegan Paul, Trench, Trubner & Co. 1898. http://history.hanover.edu/ texts/presoc/emp.htm (accessed January 28, 2008).

Flem-Ath, Rand. *When the Sky Fell: In Search of Atlantis.* New York: St. Martin's Paperbacks, 1997.

Freeman, Kathleen. *Ancilla to the Pre-Socratic Philosophers.* Cambridge, MA: Harvard University Press, 2003.

Gershenson, Daniel E. *Anaxagoras and the Birth of Scientific Method,* A Blaisdell Book in the History of Science. New York: Blaisdell Publishing, 1964.

Gorman, Vanessa B. *Miletos: The Ornament of Ionia: A History of the City to 400 BCE.* Ann Arbor, MI: University of Michigan, 2001.

Greaves, Alan M. *Miletos: A History.* London: Routledge, 2002.

Greenberg, Daniel E. and Daniel A. Gershenson. *Anaxagoras and the Birth of Physics,* Natural Philosophy before Aristotle. New York: Blaisdell Publishing, 1964.

Guthrie, W. K. C. *The Greeks and Their Gods.* Boston: Beacon Press, 1971.

Guthrie, W. K. C. *Greek Philosophers: From Thales to Aristotle.* New York: Harper Perennial, 1960.

Hadot, Ilsetraut. "The Life and Work of Simplicius in Greek and Arabic Sources." In *Aristotle Transformed: The Ancient Commentators and Their Influence,* edited by Richard Sorabji, 275–304. Ithaca, NY: Cornell University Press, 1990.

Hamilton, Edith. *Mythology.* New York: Back Bay Books, 1998.

Herodotus. *The Histories.* Book I:142. London: Penguin Classics, 2003.

Hobbs, William Herbert. *Earthquakes: An Introduction to Seismic Geology.* New York: D. Appleton and Company, 1907.

Johansen, Thomas Kjeller. *Plato's Natural Philosophy: A Study of the Timaeus-Critias.* Cambridge, UK: Cambridge University Press, 2004.

Kamminga, Harmke. "Historical Perspective: The Problem of the Origin of Life in the Context of Developments in Biology." *Origins of Life and Evolution of the Biosphere* 18 (1988): 1–11.

Kamminga, Harmke. "Life from Space: a History of Panspermia." *Vistas in Astronomy* 26 (1982): 67–86.

Kirk, Geoffrey Stephen and John Earle Raven. *Presocratic Philosophers.* Cambridge, UK: Cambridge University Press, 1984.

Lahav, Noam. *Biogenesis: Theories of Life's Origin.* Oxford, UK: Oxford University Press, 1999.

Lindberg, David C. *The Beginnings of Western Science.* Chicago: University of Chicago Press, 1992.

National Aeronautics and Space Administration. "Astrobiology." http:// astrobiology.arc.nasa.gov/ (accessed February 1, 2008).

O'Connor, J. J. and E. F. Robertson. "Simplicius." http://www-groups.dcs.st-and.ac.uk/~history/Biographies/Simplicius.html (accessed January 30, 2008).

Pillans, James. *Elements of Physical and Classical Geography.* Edinburgh: William Blackwood & Sons, 1854.

Plato. *The Last Days of Socrates.* London: Penguin Classics, 2003.

Plato. *Theaetetus.* Newburyport, MA: Focus Publishing, 2004.

Preus, Anthony. *Essays in Ancient Greek Philosophy: Before Plato,* Essays in Ancient Greek Philosophy. Albany, NY: State University of New York Press, 2001.

Preus, Antony. *Notes on Greek Philosophy from Thales to Aristotle.* Newport Pagnell, UK: Global Publications, 1997.

Raulin-Cerceau, Florence, Marie-Christie Maurel, Jean Schneider. "From Panspermia to Bioastronomy, the Evolution of the Hypothesis of Universal Life." *Origins of Life and Evolution of Biospheres* 28, no. 4– 6 (October 1998), 595–612.

Rhodes, P. J. *A History of the Classical Greek World, 478–323 BC* (Blackwell History of the Ancient World). Wiley-Blackwell, 2005. Malden, MA: Wiley-Blackwell.

Robinson, T. M. *Heraclitus.* University of Toronto Press, 1987.

Sandywell, Barry. *Presocratic Reflexivity: The Construction of Philosophical Discourse c. 600–450 BC: Logological Investigations*, vol. 3. Routledge, 1995.London: Routledge, 1995.

Schofield, Malcolm. *An Essay on Anaxagoras,* Cambridge Classical Studies. Cambridge, UK: Cambridge University Press, 1980.

Sider, David. *The Fragments of Anaxagoras*, 2nd ed. Sankt Augustin, Germany: Academic Verlag, 2005.

Simplicius. *Simplicius on Aristotle's Physics.* Ithaca, NY: Cornell University Press, 1997.

Stark, Freya. *Ionia: A Quest.* New York: Harcourt, Brace and Company, 1954.

Taylor, A. E. "On the Date of the Trial of Anaxagoras." *The Classical Quarterly* 11, no. 2. (April 1917): 81–87.

Robert Temple, "The Prehistory of Panspermia: Astrophysical or Metaphysical?" *International Journal of Astrobiology*, vol. 6, no. 2, April 2007, pp. 169–180.

Teodorsson, Sven-Tage. *Anaxagoras' Theory of Matter.* Atlantic Highlands, NJ: Humanities Publishing, 1983.

Theodossious, E., P. G. Niarchos, V. N. Manimanis, and W. Orchiston. "The Fall of a Meteorite at Aegos Potami in 467/6 BC." *Journal of Astronomical History and Heritage* 5, no. 2 (2002): 135–140.

Thucydides. *The History of the Peloponnesian War.* Translated by William Smith. New York: Harper & Brothers, 1855.

Turner, William. "Ionian School of Philosophy." Transcribed by Tomas Hancil. *The Catholic Encyclopedia*, vol. 8. New York: Robert Appleton Company, 1910. http://www.newadvent.org/cathen/08092a.htm (accessed January 26, 2008).

Vlastos, Gregory. "One World or Many in Anaxagoras?" In *Studies in Presocratic Philosophy. International Library of Philosophy and Scientific Method,* vol. 2. *Eleatics and Pluralists*, edited by R. E. Allen and David J. Furley, 354–360. Atlantic Highlands, NJ: Humanities Press, 1975.

Vlastos, Gregory. "The Physical Theory of Anaxagoras." In *Studies in Presocratic Philosophy. International Library of Philosophy and Scientific Method.* vol. 2. *Eleatics and Pluralists,* edited by R. E. Allen and David J. Furley, 323–353. Atlantic Highlands, NJ: Humanities Press, 1975.

Woodbury, Leonard. "Anaxagoras and Athens." *Phoenix* 35, no. 4 (Winter 1981): 295–315.

Zabinkova, N. N. "Generic Names Ending in -ma and Family Names Derived from Them." *Taxon* 14, no. 6 (July 1965): 184–187.

978-0-595-49596-
0-595-49596-6

Lightning Source UK Ltd.
Milton Keynes UK
17 September 2009

143863UK00001B/54/P